HIKING TRAILS
OF THE
SUNSHINE COAST

HIKING TRAILS
of the
SUNSHINE COAST

Rita Percheson, Pam Gross
and Sandy Barrett
Illustrations Robert Jack

A JOINT HARBOUR PUBLISHING/
SIGNPOST BOOKS PUBLICATION

ISBN 0-913140-41-4 (U.S.)
ISBN 0-920080-32-4 (Canada)

Preparation of this book was financed in part by the Local Initiatives Programme of the Government of Canada by arrangement with the Sunshine Coast Regional District.

The authors wish to thank Lester Peterson, Leslie Black, Barb Laakso, Tom Sheldon, the B.C. Forest Service (Sechelt Office), John Hind-Smith and many others who helped bring this book about.

Published jointly in the U.S. and Canada by:
    Harbour Publishing, P.O. Box 119, Madeira Park, B.C. V0N 2H0 (Canada)
    Signpost Books, 8912 192nd S.W., Edmonds, Washington 98020 (U.S.)

Printed for the publishers by Pulp Press.

Design by Robert Jack. Cover photo by Howard White.

MADE IN CANADA.

Table of Contents

FOREWORD

A covey of smooth stones wing out skipping across the wrinkled calm of the bay and you turn to see the small browned faces squinting against the delicious sun. You're a kid again too and hunting for that perfect flat stone with a balanced weight to win against the waves.

In the moist coolness beside a forest stream you watch for darker shadows purposeful in the current; next time you'll bring a rod. This time it's good enough to chill your bones on the willing moss; and the shadows grow bolder.

From the mountain you can see it all, the crazy weavings of the coastline hemming the rich green, and lakes splashed everywhere, and snowy peaks behind you forever, and you think maybe mountain-climbers aren't really lunatics after all.

This is the Sunshine Coast of British Columbia, one of the best recreational areas the province has to offer.

While many know the coast for its sportfishing, swimming, and other ocean related attractions, little has been said about the variety of hiking trails here.

In this book we have concentrated on the area between Port Melon and Earl's Cove, covering twenty hikes for people of all ages and abilities. Also included at the back is hiking information for the hard-core stompers, long may they live.

The Sunshine Coast is an incredibly beautiful place to live or visit, and we encountered sad grumblings over the influx of debeautifiers this book might occasion. In response we painted a picture of the hiker: considerate, responsible, non-littering and generally ecology-minded. Please live up to your image.

There is a limit to the amount of detail it is practical to give in a general guidebook such as this, especially because the country it covers is open, wild and changing. With but few exceptions the trails and ski-routes discussed here are informal ones not marked with elegantly chiselled wooden signposts or even flimsy plastic flagging. Worse, the logging roads often used for reference are constantly being abandoned and added to. We have done our best to tell you what is out there and set you off in the right direction, but picking out the exact route to follow and getting there safely is entirely up to you. So watch your step and use your noodle.

THE BASICS

GARBAGE: Nowadays people shouldn't need to be reminded about littering but small scraps of gum wrappers and cigarette butts often miss your attention only to catch the next hiker's.

CAMPFIRES: Hopefully Smokey the Bear inundated all hikers with campfire awareness before he and his hat passed on to the Eternal Blueberry Patch. Keep a cleared area around your fire and when you think it's thouroughly out stir the remains with your hand to check for secret embers.

FOOTGEAR: Strong shoes or hiking boots are of prime importance to a hiker's wardrobe. If you do decide to invest in a new pair of hiking boots here are several tips to consider:

The height of hiking boots is important as those much higher than six inches may chafe your leg or prevent your ankle from bending comfortably.

Gussets should fit snugly to keep the water out and tongues should be padded, especially at the top where you lean into them.

Runners may be great for nimble-footing about but they give you sore feet and bruised anklebones when hiking. The stiff sole of a hiking boot keeps rocks from bruising your feet and the stiffness of the leather uppers keeps you from twisting your ankles. The degree of stiffness of a hiking boot is measured in weight; with a lightweight boot good for paved sidewalks. Mediumweight boots are the most common, good for trail and snow hiking. Heavyweight boots are used by the real climbers of rock and ice.

Waterproof your boots thoroughly and regularly, rubbing the waterproofing compound well into all seams. And never dry your boots too close to a fire, the leather will shrink.

Two tricks for easier hiking: if your heel moves up and down too much inside your boot while walking uphill you will blister. Avoid walking on the balls of your feet, walk flatfooted and you'll avoid blisters and have a better grip of the hill. To prevent your toes from stubbing against the front of the boot on a long or steep downhill, lace your boots up tighter. It really works.

COMPASS: One of the handiest inventions we'll ever own is our compass. You can buy a good compass for around ten dollars, and learn how to use it in twenty minutes. However, we have designed our maps so you don't need a compass but if you do have one take it along for practice.

HUNTERS: Watch out for them. Wear an article of bright clothing and leave your drinking hat with the bunny ears at home during hunting season.

LOGGING ROADS: Many of our hikes make use of the local logging roads. Logging companies throughout the province suffer at the hands of vandals lighting fires and damaging machinery. The less trouble occasioned on their roads the more amenable they will be to leaving gates open in future.

GRADING THE HIKES

We have graded each hike according to its relative difficulty so that you won't inadvertently send your grandmother scrambling up a mountain. Or, if she's in better shape than you, send you unwittingly after her.

This grading system is only to give you a general idea of the hike, and it is important that you read the description of each hike to obtain a clearer picture of distances, hiking times, terrain and hazards.

PRIMARY: These hikes are the easiest ones, suitable for young children or for those who merely want a pleasant walk. Also, they usually take the least time.

INTERMEDIATE: These are the medium hikes—good for the exercise and all that jazz.

ADVANCED: And these are the toughies that drag you up mountains and down into the middle of nowhere. They give you a great sense of accomplishment and a big appetite. Don't be daunted. If we three made it. . .

LEGEND

★	HIKE BEGINS
▬▬▬▬	HIGHWAY & PAVED ROADS
────	GRAVEL & LOGGING ROADS
- - - -	TRAILS
～～	CREEKS
≈≈≈	CREEKS ~ LARGE SCALE
▬	LAKES
～～	OCEAN
◈	WATERFALLS
⌂	LOGGED OFF AREA
▥	BRIDGE
†	CEMETERY
⌂	SMALL BUILDING
冂	HYDRO LINE
⛺	TENTING

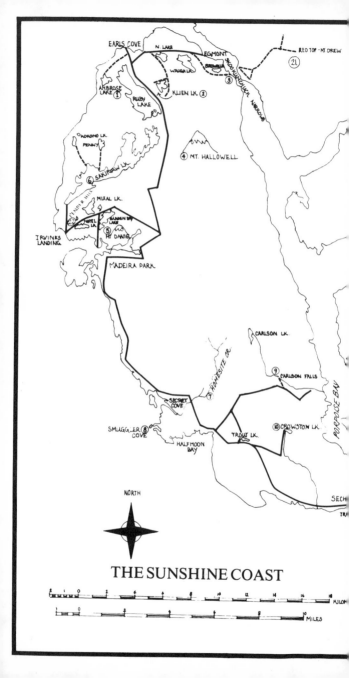

THE SUNSHINE COAST

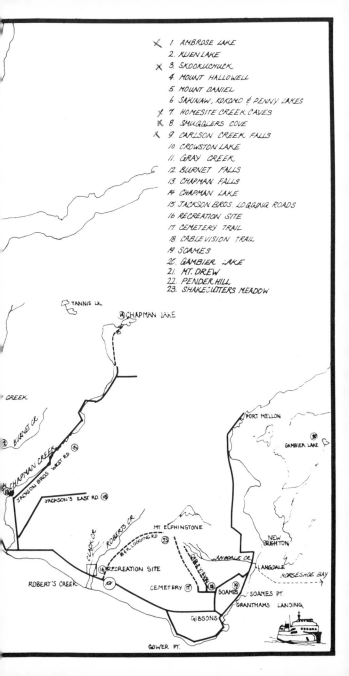

1. AMBROSE LAKE
2. KLEIN LAKE
3. SKOOKUCHUCK
4. MOUNT HALLOWELL
5. MOUNT DANIEL
6. SAKINAW, KOKOMO & PENNY LAKES
7. HOMESITE CREEK CAVES
8. SMUGGLERS COVE
9. CARLSON CREEK FALLS
10. CROWSTON LAKE
11. GRAY CREEK
12. BURNET FALLS
13. CHAPMAN FALLS
14. CHAPMAN LAKE
15. JACKSON BROS. LOGGING ROADS
16. RECREATION SITE
17. CEMETERY TRAIL
18. CABLE VISION TRAIL
19. SOAMES
20. GAMBIER LAKE
21. MT. DREW
22. PENDER HILL
23. SHAKECUTTERS MEADOW

AMBROSE LAKE ECOLOGICAL RESERVE

ACCESS: Take Highway 101 from Earl's Cove ferry terminal about 1500 feet to the Cove Cay Estates road, which is the first on your right (south) side. From here take Timberline Road to the right and follow it to its end at the hydro line.

HIKING TIME: One hour into Ambrose Lake, which is 1½ miles from the end of Timberline Road.

DESCRIPTION: Primary to Intermediate. The way to Ambrose Lake is along another of those delightful retired logging roads, all overgrown with quiet grass. There are several forks in the road so watch your map as you go.

POINTS OF INTEREST: The cool dampness of this mossy road provides the perfect climate for wild violets, and these delicate yellow flowers are sprinkled along the roadway with even a few of the less common purple variety found closer to the lake. The road runs close to the ocean and at some points the rich blue waters of Agamemnon Channel can be seen. In the background the lazyday drone of winders making the logbooms off Nelson Island can be heard.

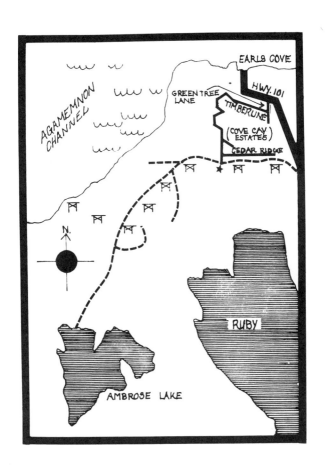

AMBROSE LAKE

Ambrose Lake is in the middle of a large ecological reserve set aside for scientific study, and the whole area abounds with deer, raccoons, and other wild animals. The lake itself features a unique bog ecology with hoardes of frogs and other marsh creatures inhabiting its shores. It is also a favourite haunt for loons, whose weird cries can be heard vibrating over the quiet lake.

Roger Wilcox photo.

Beaver pond near Klein Lakes. Robertson Wood photo.

Klein Lake. Robertson Wood photo.

KLEIN LAKE

ACCESS: Follow Egmont Road from Highway 101 for one mile until you come to the North Lake Road turn-off. The turn-off, which is not marked, runs along the south side of the lake.

HIKING TIME: 1½ hours into Klein Lake which is 2½ miles from the Egmont Road.

DESCRIPTION: Primary to intermediate. The beginning portion of the hike following the lakeshore runs through a small area of summer homes. The road, part of an old logging operation, then veers away from North Lake and heads up to Klein Lake, which is the centre of a large ecological reserve. A small marshy lake is passed ¼ mile before reaching Klein Lake.

POINTS OF INTEREST: On the western end of the small marshy lake, where a stream runs in, beavers have constructed a dam. This little lake is also a haven for wild ducks as there is an extensive patch of marsh reeds at one end.

Klein Lake, with its intriguing shape, is known as a good canoeing lake and in the summer is also good for swimming. Its plentitude of fish make it a favorite with kingfishers, whose bold blue wings can be seen flashing across the water from spring to fall.

The south-western shore has several grassy clearings for camping.

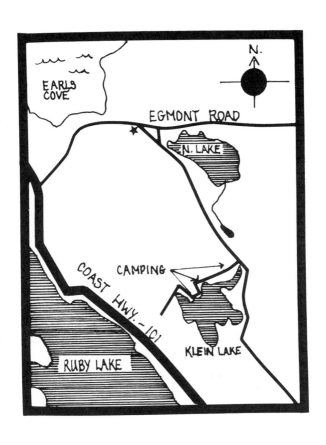

KLEIN LAKE

SKOOKUMCHUCK RAPIDS

ACCESS: Take the Egmont Road approximately 100 feet from Egmont and, on your left, you will see a gravelled parking area with a park sign marking the entrance.

HIKING TIME: One hour to Roland Point which is two and a half miles from the parking lot.

DESCRIPTION: Primary. This trail was built by the Parks and Recreation Branch and is well cleared. Direction and information signs and public toilets are located along the trail, though campfires are not permitted.

POINTS OF INTEREST: "Skookumchuck" is an old Indian name meaning "Strong Waters", almost an understatement when one considers that these are one of the West Coast's largest salt water rapids. The tales concerning these rapids are many and tragic, for though the channel appears calm at slack tide, when the tide turns a twenty foot boat can be sucked down into the cavernous whirlpools. On a ten foot tide two hundred billion gallons of water churn through the narrow shallow channel.

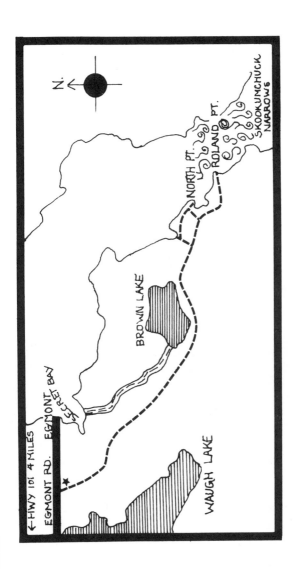

SKOOKUMCHUCK

The rapids occur off North Point on the outgoing tide and off Roland Point on the incoming tide, with the best waterfall action also on the incoming tide. One hour after slack water the Skookumchuck is at its peak, so a tide chart should be consulted if you want to get the best show. Slack water is determined by adding one hour and 45 minutes to the change in tide (under Point Atkinson in the tidebook) and then adding a further 5 minutes for every foot of change. That is, if low tide is 4 feet and high tide is 14 feet, there is 10 feet of change and slack water will be 5 × 10 = 50 minutes plus one hour and 45 minutes, or 2 hours and 35 minutes after low tide.

The best show is on the rising tide and the more feet of change in the tide the better the show. When low tide is 9 feet and high tide is 11 feet not much happens, but when low tide is − 2 feet and high tide is 15 feet the earth shakes.

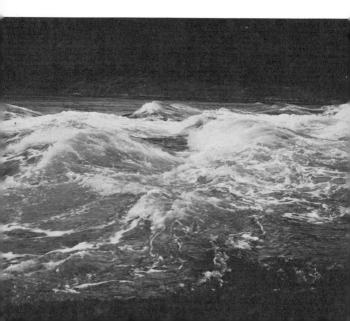

At low tide the bays reveal a colourful display of sea life, with giant barnacles, colonies of sea urchins, sea anemones, moluscs, and others. The action of the current causes these creatures to grow to extravagant sizes, and local fishermen prize the narrows for its abundance of salmon and cod.

The wealth of marine life in this area has made it a favourite with scuba divers, who come from all over the west coast to dive in these waters. One local diver showed us slides of taming an octopus, an animal he described as "friendly as a puppy" once it knows you won't hurt it!

HAZARDS: The utmost caution must be exercised on the rocks overlooking the rapids as there is no hope of rescuing anyone who falls in. When we were small children our parents would tie us to trees by a long rope to prevent any tragedies befalling us.

Skookumchuck Trail. Stephen Jackson photo.

◀ **Skookumchuck Rapids.** Stephen Jackson photo.

RED TOP (MOUNT DREW)

ACCESS: Red Top (Mount Drew) is one of the most accessible 6,200-foot mountains you're going to find anywhere but at that it's a bit more of a challenge than others listed here. First you must get to Egmont, (see the Skookumchuck Trail) then you must arrange a ride across the inlet, either to the Argus Aggregates gravel pit or the S & W logging camp inside Skookumchick Rapids. Enquiries can be made at Bathgate's Store, Egmont Marina, Jervis View Marina or by button-holing a likely-looking local on the government dock. Once safely landed on the north side of the inlet, simply point yourself towards Red Top and start walking. The road is many-branched, but the main route up is fairly obvious. One newer branch leads to the rockslide at the base of Red Top which affords the most direct route to the peak while a disused branch leads to the unnamed peak west of Red Top. The longer and more interesting route is to go up this lesser peak and cross the high plateau which gives access to the north side of Red Top. The best time to try it is from July to late September.

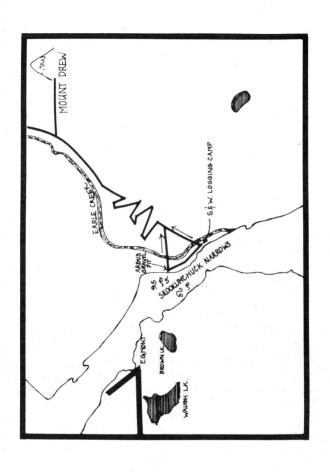

RED TOP (MOUNT DREW)

HIKING TIME: One to three days. The road to the base rises through ten miles of spectacularly ugly logging slash and is just as steep as they could make it. On foot and with a pack this calls for a full day's exertion in itself, and if someone in a pickup truck offers you a lift you won't miss a thing by taking it. Trail bikes would be another perfectly acceptable solution, and some locals have gone so far as to have their four-wheel drives ferried over by the local landing barge. Once at the foot of the rockslide, the peak can be reached in an hour and a half.

DESCRIPTION: Advanced. This is a climb, not a hike, and should be attempted only by the sure of foot.

POINTS OF INTEREST: Too many to mention. Like the Black Tusk in Garibaldi Park, Red Top is a real mountain which brings that heady Olympian realm normally reserved for the serious alpinist within the grasp of your ordinary tax-paying hockey fan.

Standing in the clear as it does, Red Top offers a panoramic view of the Sunshine Coast. Looking southwest, the Sechelt Peninsula lays small and whole in the foreground with the glittering expanse of Georgia Strait and the mountains of Vancouver Island beyond. The outlook to the north and west reveals Jervis Inlet twisting its way out of the Coast Range toward Malaspina Strait and Texada Island. Turning to the east, it seems almost as if you could kick a rock down into Narrows Inlet, and you would need a map, compass and the geographical instincts of Captain Cook to sort the towering rows of inland peaks into their respective ranges.

27

The north side of the peak is home to a small glacier, the sheer face of which local climbers have at times put to use as a 1,000-foot slide, protecting the seats of their jeans with a sheet of plastic film. Later in the season the upper edge of the glacier becomes honeycombed with ice caves which some climbers have explored and lived to tell about, but of course such adventures can only be recommended for those with strong suicidal urges. The shoulder laying west of the peak has a small pool with drinkable water near its western edge and makes for good overnight camping if you decide to stay and explore more of the surrounding alpine plateau which would take many visits to do fully.

The reason for the local name "Red Top" becomes clearer after a visit to the mountain, which is composed entirely of a loose rusty-red, iron-bearing rock. The formation is rich in many minerals and has been the object of much claim-staking in the past though no development has ever been undertaken. The area is barren except for low alpine shrubs, some scrub in the hollows and alpine rodents such as rabbits and marmots.

HAZARDS: The road is actively used by logging equipment and courtesy if not self-preservation demands one clear one's plans at the S & W camp before proceeding. A bonus of such action might be the offer of a ride up the hill, although this isn't to be counted on. The man to talk to if he's available is camp owner Howard Stromquist, who is a very approachable and considerate individual. Once launched upon the climb, WATCH FOR FALLING ROCK. If you don't end up riding a boulder over the edge yourself, you may end up braining a valued friend. Keep your party staggered so you don't wipe each other out with mini-rockslides. In this country you either use your head or you won't have one to use.

H. White

Red Top (Mount Drew). Robertson Wood photo.

MOUNT HALLOWELL

ACCESS: Take Highway 101 from Garden Bay Road ½ mile. 1000 feet past the Pender Harbour Secondary School take the first road on your right, on the opposite side of the highway from the school.

HIKING TIME: Four hours up to the end of the logging road just past a little lake, which is five miles from the highway. From here it is another 1½ miles, another hour, up to the Forestry lookout if you decide to climb that last knoll. Elevation 4100 feet.

DESCRIPTION: Intermediate to Advanced. Those hikers who have been up to the lookout have usually made this an overnight hike. The climb up is long and steep, but the view is the best on the coast.

Unfortunately the trail to the lookout from the end of the logging road is difficult to find in spots, and has now been partially obscured by a new logging show operating on the back slopes of the mountain. If you do want to reach the lookout you'll have to hunt for the trail or just make your own way up.

POINTS OF INTEREST: Once you reach the top you can look down over Agamemnon Channel and the Strait of Georgia. Behind you is Sechelt Inlet, Narrows Inlet, and Jervis Inlet, so you get a 360 degree view perched up on the very top. It really is inspiring.

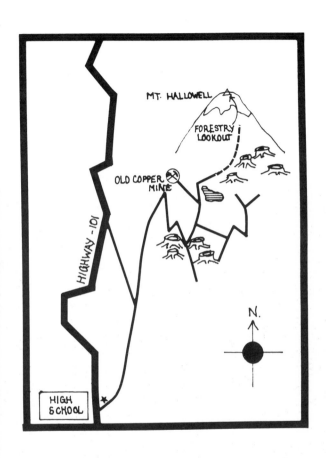

MOUNT HALLOWELL

View west from Mount Hallowell. Ruby Lake in left foreground with Agamemnon Channel and Nelson Island in middle ground. Jervis Inlet and mainland Shore beyond. B.C. Forest Service photo.

MOUNT DANIEL

ACCESS: Take Garden Bay Road from Highway 101 two miles to the old garbage dump road. This road is not marked but it is the first on your left after Oyster Bay Road.

HIKING TIME: One hour to the top, which is 1½ miles from Garden Bay Road. The descent takes somewhat less time.

DESCRIPTION: Intermediate. This old logging road takes a fairly direct route up the mountain and is easily followed, though whippy young alders are crowding the roadbed. The only part of the road that is difficult to find is near the beginning, just past the area of stumps. Follow the map closely to find the entrance to the trail through the alders. Just before the top of the road, which is also the top of the western peak, you will see a fifty foot rock bluff to your left. We suggest you make your own way up this bluff to take full advantage of the view.

POINTS OF INTEREST: The eastern peak of Mount Daniel was for years the scene of puberty rites practiced by the Sechelt Indian maidens. At the time of puberty these girls were isolated to the mountain top for four months. During this time communication with the rest of the tribe was cut off, except for the daily visit of the older women bringing food.

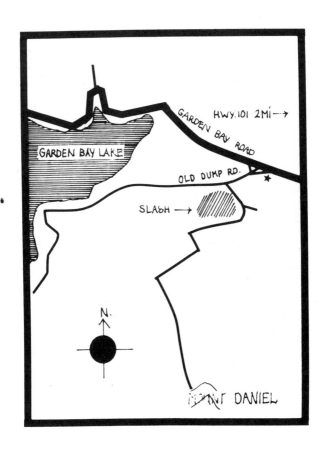

MOUNT DANIEL

Looking west over Pender Harbour from Mount Daniel. John Hind-Smith photo.

While in isolation these girls used smooth stones to construct large circles twenty to thirty feet across. These circles, called "Moon Rings", were symbolic of the moon. The Indians' beliefs were strongly involved with that planet's influence. Every evening at dusk a girl would begin her ritual with her Moon Ring, lifting each stone in turn and talking to it as though it were the moon. By dawn each stone would have had its turn and the ritual was finished. Evidence of these rings can still be seen on the mossy peak.

Mary Saul, a local Indian woman who participated in these rites as a girl, smiled at her recollections of conversion to Catholicism. For her the transition was easy, as telling a rosary was so similar to the Moon Ring ritual!

The young men of the tribe also had similar rituals which they performed in isolation on Mount Cecil.

Their constructions of stones were in the form of serpents, symbolic of fatherhood.

Mount Daniel has two peaks, with the old logging road winding up the west peak. The eastern peak, with its fascinating history, has no trail though several people have climbed up its side from Oyster Bay Road.

From the western peak a splendid view of the many lakes, inlets, and islands can be enjoyed. Directly below is Garden Bay Lake which was sacred to the young Indian women. Katherine Lake, Mixal Lake, and the intriguing coastline of Pender Harbour can also be seen.

PENDER HILL

ACCESS: Turn off Highway 101 onto Garden Bay Road, turn off Garden Bay Road onto Irvines Landing Road, drive down Irvines Landing Road to Lee Road. The trail up Pender Hill starts on the north side of Irvines Landing Road about 200 feet east of Lee Road, precisely opposite a private driveway leading down to an older-style home with a steeply pitched roof.

HIKING TIME: Half an hour going up, 15 minutes coming down.
DESCRIPTION: Intermediate. Short but steep.

POINTS OF INTEREST: For the time it takes this may be the most rewarding little jaunt of them all. In the days when Pender Harbour served as a winter quarters for the entire Sechelt Indian nation and in fact boasted a larger population than it does today, this was the lookout preferred by sentries on the watch for parties of Yaculta or Haida war canoes, which might be expected to break into the clear around Cape Cockburn any moment of any day. Although only half as high as nearby Mount Daniel, Pender Hill affords a clearer and more comprehensive view of the Pender Harbour area in its relation to surrounding waters and it is much more quickly scaled. For the same reasons it makes the best place for visitors to get an overview of the area's famous "drowned landscape" today or for locals to climb free of the claustrophobic ruts of their everyday and restore the broad perspective. You can sit for hours beside the bronze Geodesic Survey plate cemented into the top of the dome and watch trollers and plodding tugboats, luxury cruisers and streaking outboards come and go as the busiest harbour on the Sunshine Coast goes about its day.

Not the least of the attractions of Pender Hill is its terrain: on the east side is a cliff so breathtakingly sheer it seems you could take a modest leap and land in the cool green waters of Hotel Lake directly below (don't try it). The entire area on top is open, gently benched and carpeted with acres of cushiony moss that can bring the somersaulting kid out of the tiredest old bones. The west slope supports what must be the nearest thing you'll ever see to an "arbutus forest" and the top is rich in the relatively rare "hairy manzanita," a type of miniature bush arbutus with bright red bark. You will also find it a good place to replenish your supply of wild herbs such as yarrow, juniper berry, kinnikinnik, and in season such flowering plants as wild violets, wild onion, tiger and chocolate lily give the area the appearance of a vast rock garden. And that funny noise you hear isn't a bemused fellow hiker crouching behind a bush blowing into a beerbottle, it's one of the hill's multitudinous male blue grouse calling to his mate. Don't let this give you any ideas though—Pender Hill is within the Sunshine Coast Regional District's firearm restriction zone.

All in all, a perfect place for picnic on a summer day with a cool ocean breeze or an overnight campout under a full moon.

HAZARDS: Loose rock and slippery moss.

SAKINAW LAKE, KOKOMO LAKE, AND PENNY LAKE (CANOE AND HIKE)

ACCESS: Take the Garden Bay Road exit off Highway 101 and then turn onto the Irvines Landing Road at Garden Bay Lake. Next, turn right on Lee's Road and follow this road to the end at Sakinaw Lake.

HIKING TIME: Sakinaw Lake is eight miles in length and is a suitable paradise for canoers. The southwestern tip of the lake can be reached by canoe and, from here, it is only a ten minute walk to the ocean. There are also good trails leading into Kokomo and Penny Lake, which are about a mile in and half an hour hiking each way.

DESCRIPTION: Primary to Intermediate. The trail to the ocean is an old logging road on land owned by the Sechelt Indian Band and permission must be obtained from them before taking the walk. The closest island is a provincial park and has a cleared area in the centre for camping.

POINTS OF INTEREST: Directly across the lake from the end of Lee's Road are sheer cliffs with Indian rock paintings dating back at least to the nineteenth century. The painting of these symbolic figures was a yearly ritual of the local Sechelt

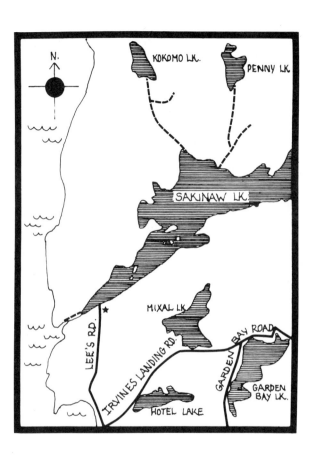

SAKINAW LAKE AREA

Maple in blossom. Brian Blackwell photo.

Pictographs at Sakinaw Lake. Roger Wilcox photo.

Indians. Their medicine man recorded these figures as they appeared to him in halucinatory dreams induced by rubbing leaves from the "ay-yahl-ay-wahn" plant on his forehead. The layers of pigment applied to the granite over the years have left an impression which will last well into the future.

As part of the maturity rites of their tribe, the young men had to swim underwater across the lake at this point, coming up under the rock paintings. The trial was made doubly fearful as the Indians believed the lake was inhabited by a serpent. If it happens to be a hot summer day when you're here, you might try the underwater swim—it's only about ¼ mile.

Dusk on Sakinaw Lake. Roger Wilcox photo.

The lakeshore itself is rather sparsely populated with summer homes, as most are accessible by boat only. Numerous small islands provide choice swimming spots and the lake is well stocked with cutthroat trout. Local fishermen claim a gang lure is the best tackle for catching these fish. Sakinaw is an extremely deep lake, just over 1000 feet in some places. As these lower portions are well below sea level they are salt water, and even support oceanic growth.

A scant 700 feet of land separates the southwestern tip of the lake from the ocean, and here a stream runs out. The trail to the beach follows this stream, and evidence of beavers is seen in the gnawed tree trunks along the banks. Closer to the stream's mouth, the Fish & Wildlife Branch have built fish ladders for spawning sockeye.

Homesite Creek. Roger Wilcox photo.

HOMESITE CREEK CAVES

ACCESS: Take Highway 101 west from Sechelt 6-8/10 miles. The turnoff road is the second road on the north side of the highway 1-3/10 miles past Brooks Road, and has to be closely watched for. Follow this turnoff road one mile up to the cut off for the picnic site and trail as marked on the map.

HIKING TIME: One half hour for the circle route which is one mile long.

DESCRIPTION: Primary. This trail is well-defined except for that portion that runs around the pond, where you may have to consult your map to pick up the trail again. Numerous small trails in the picnic site area lead to the creek or just twine through the woods.

POINTS OF INTEREST: Nicknamed the "Gumdrop Caves" for their small size, these twelve limestone caves are one of the highlights of this hike. The two largest caves are around forty feet long and are inhabited by large cave crickets.

The B.C. Forestry has provided picnic tables and cleared areas for campfires near a waterfall and further down the creek a log jam has created a tempting swimming hole.

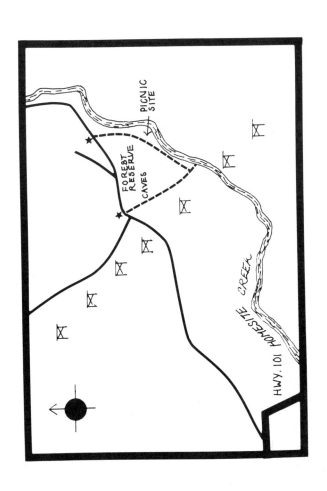

PICNIC SITE

FOREST RESERVE CAVES

HOMESITE CREEK

HWY. 101

HOMESITE CREEK CAVES

SMUGGLERS COVE MARINE PARK

ACCESS: Take Highway 101 from Sechelt 5-1/2 miles to Brooks Road. Brooks Road is on your left going up a long hill just past Halfmoon Bay. Follow Brooks Road miles to its end, making sure you don't take a wrong turning along one of the subdivision roads. The small parking lot for hikers is 1000 feet from the end of Brooks Road.

HIKING TIME: Twenty minutes into Smugglers Cove which is a scant mile from Brooks Road. Plans to build more trails are now being drawn and signs will be posted in the park when they are complete.

DESCRIPTION: Primary. For years Smugglers Cove Marine Park has been accessible by boat only and the trail in is just now being properly cleared.

With its narrow mouth and deceptive length, Smugglers Cove has proved a perfect harbour for illegal marine traffic, from which it derived its name.

After the completion of the Canadian Pacific Railway in the last century thousands of Chinese workers were left unemployed. These workers were not allowed to immigrate into the States so an illegal business of running them across the border developed.

A man known as Pirate Kelly was one of the main traffickers in Chinese, and Smugglers Cove was his hideout. From there he would sail the workers down

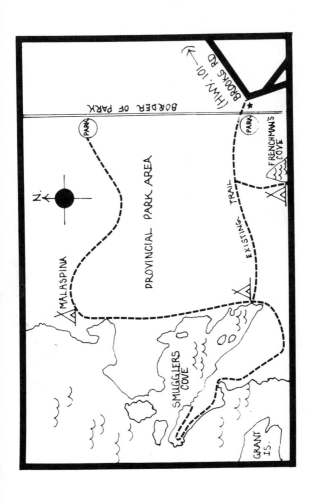

SMUGGLER'S COVE MARINE PARK

Smuggler's Cove. John Hind-Smith photo.

through the Gulf Islands and into the States. To avoid detection he had been known to throw his entire Chinese cargo overboard, all roped to an anchor!

Pirate's Rock off the south-western tip of Thormanby Island was also named after him.

Smugglers Cove again lived up to its name in the 1920's during Prohibition when a large still was manufacturing hootch on Texada Island. From Texada it was run into Sugglers Cove and then down across the line.

Future plans for the park include camping facilities, more trails, and boat moorage.

The waters along this part of the coast are also good for skin and scuba diving. Brooks Cove, Frenchman's Cove and Pirate Rock are particularly colourful.

HAZARDS: Pirate Kelly's grandchildren...

50

Nudibranch. Tom Sheldon photo.

Coarse sea anemones. Tom Sheldon photo.

CARLSON CREEK WATERFALL

ACCESS: Take Highway 101 from Sechelt seven miles to Trout Lake Road, at the bottom of the long hill before Halfmoon Bay. (Ignore the Trout Lake Road that starts just past the lake.) Follow Trout Lake Road one mile up to where it runs right alongside another road, Doyle's Logging Road. Switch over to Doyle's Logging Road and follow it another mile to a junction of three roads. Take the road furthest right, heading east.

HIKING TIME: 1-1/2 hour into the falls, which are 3-1/2 miles from the junction of the three logging roads. If you risk your car along the right fork at the junction as far as the trail you will save 2-1/2 miles and just over an hour.

DESCRIPTION: Primary. This old logging road is reasonably level right in to the falls. Young alders encroaching on its borders and grass down the middle make it a favourite haunt of grouse.

POINTS OF INTEREST: At the bridge crossing Carlson Creek you can look down over the double set of falls, but to get the best view you should make your way down the bank to the bottom. And the pool at the base is not too chilly for swimming. Carlson Lake is a warm, shallow lake, hence Carlson Creek is also reasonably warm.

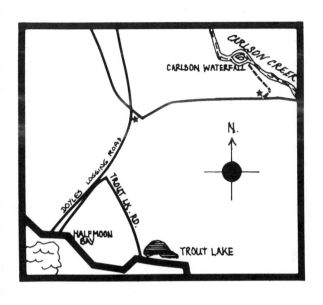

CARLSON CREEK FALLS

CROWSTON LAKE

ACCESS: Take Highway 101 west from the flashing red intersection light in Sechelt 6-8/10 miles. The entrance road is 1/4 mile east of Trout Lake on the upper side of the highway. The road is cut into the hillside and veers off at a forty-five degree angle.

HIKING TIME: One and a half hours into Crowston Lake which is three miles from the highway. Allow equal time for return.

DESCRIPTION: Primary. This trail is an old logging road which follows a gentle incline up to the lake. It is important to note that the turn-off for the lake is the first on the right-hand (east) after the log bridge. The lake itself is not clearly visible from the western or northern shores until the campsite is reached. We found water-proof footwear a must as small streams traverse the road at various points and large puddles are formed.

POINTS OF INTEREST: Children can pursue one of their favorite pastimes when, at certain times of the year, frogs and salamanders abound in the puddles along the trail. Although the lake is not that suitable for swimming due to the marshy nature of the lakeshore, it has a cleared camping site on the northern edge from which to enjoy the lake's serenity.

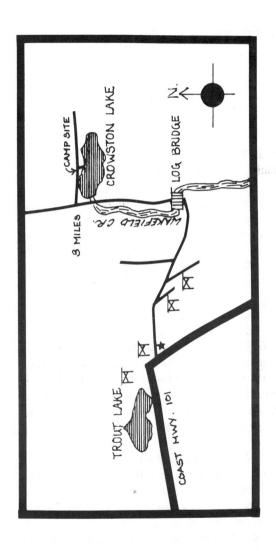

CROWSTON LAKE

GRAY CREEK

ACCESS: Take the East Porpoise Bay Road from the flashing red intersection light in Sechelt 5-4/10 miles. Gray Creek traverses the road at the third bridge from Sechelt, three hundred feet after the blacktop gives way to a gravel road surface. Tuwanek is only one-half mile further down the road.

HIKING TIME: Fifteen minutes to the first set of falls and another fifteen minutes to the second set, which is 3/4 of a mile from the road. Allow equal time for return.

DESCRIPTION: Primary to Intermediate. Closely following the creek, the trail is level and easily hiked to the first set of falls. From here the trail proceeds along a fallen log and is not so clearly defined. This is another trail that can be soggy during the rainy season so wear your puddle-jumpers!

POINTS OF INTEREST: Along the entire length of this beautiful creek are myriad trout pools and waterfalls. Old campfires along the trail bear testimony to the sizzling feasts enjoyed by fishermen. In the middle of the second set of falls is a large rock outcropping for suntanning and enjoying the view of the cascades.

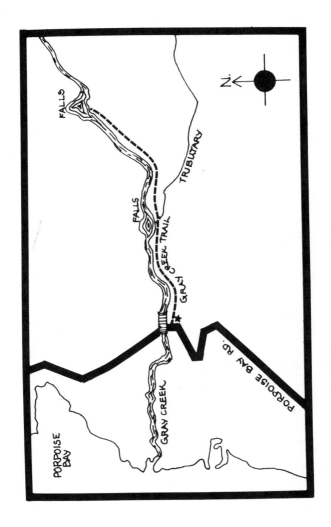

GRAY CREEK TRAIL

Gray Creek is the only major unlogged creek on the Sunshine Coast and the old forest along its banks is draped with spanish moss, or "witch's hair", lending an enchanted tone to the trail.

HAZARDS: Small children should be supervised around the waterfalls as the rocks can be slippery.

Oyster Mushrooms. Roger Wilcox photo.

BURNET FALLS

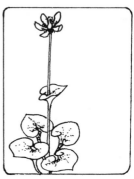

ACCESS: Take the East Porpoise Bay Road from the flashing red intersection light in Sechelt two miles. Pass Swanson's gravel pit on your right and then Porpoise Bay Campsites on your left. The access road takes off up a hill at the next corner, about 1000 feet past the campsite sign. This is a junction for three roads so check your map closely.

HIKING TIME: Fifteen minutes to the falls, which are 3/8 mile from the highway.

DESCRIPTION: Primary. Starting out the trail follows an old logging road which later gives way to a footpath. Just before the end of the trail, a barely discernible path heads down the bank to the creek.

POINTS OF INTEREST: While this isn't much of a hike, really only a fifteen minute walk, it does take you to a quiet and secluded spot. If your enthusiasm for awe-inspiring cataracts, treacherous rapids, and towering mountains is waning, try these unpretentious falls to refresh your spirit.

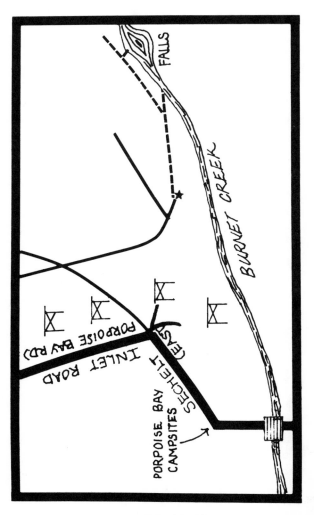

BURNET CREEK

The end of the trail high on the bank opposite Burnet Falls provides a good vantage point, but there is another trail down to the creek bed. Beside the creek a little gravel beach extends, just below a log jam that creates a swirling black pool underneath the falls. Dogwoods and ferns overhang the banks; and oregon grape, or Indian popcorn as it is sometimes called, line the trail.

Roger Wilcox photo. ▶

CHAPMAN FALLS

ACCESS: Take Highway 101 east from the flashing red intersection light in Sechelt one mile to the Selma Park Road. Going up the Selma Park Road take the first road on your left and follow it to the hydro line. Take the road along the hydro line to your right, about two blocks, until you reach the ravine. The trail takes off down the bank just past the last hydro pole on the west bank of the ravine.

HIKING TIME: One hour to Chapman Falls, which is one and three-quarters miles from the hydro line.

DESCRIPTION: Primary to Intermediate. The steep part of the trail is right at its beginning where stairs had to be cut into the bank, but the rest is just good old trail!

POINTS OF INTEREST: Chapman Creek has many large pools which provide excellent steelhead fishing in the spring, and also has numerous small waterfalls down its entire length. The view of the large double falls can be enjoyed from a cleared picnic site at the trail's end, and it's worth packing your camera in for photos of these misty cascades.

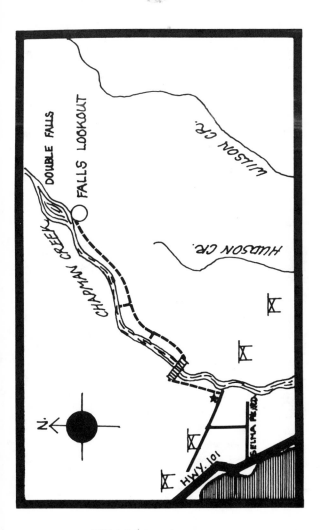

CHAPMAN FALLS

Our friends Roger and company, who cleared this trail, have built a great single log bridge across the creek. One of our few regrets is that we neglected to take any photos of Roger's escapades while constructing this bridge. He had to fell the tree across the creek and then inch out along it to cut the branches off and add the railing. However, we're sure you'll appreciate his daring when you see the bridge.

HAZARDS: The area past the falls is closed to the public as it is the watershed for the area.

Bridge on Chapman Creek. Author photo.

Lower falls, Chapman Creek. Ian Corrance photo.

CHAPMAN LAKE

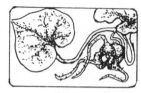

ACCESS: Take Highway 101 east from Sechelt to the Jackson Bros. Logging office in Wilson Creek. Across the highway, to the east of the Homestead Drive-In is Jacksons' Logging Road. There is a large sign at the entrance which reads "Logging Road Do Not Enter" . . . this is the right road. Follow this logging road one mile up to the junction at the hydro line and from there take the "West Road". From here it is another eleven miles to the top of the road where the trail begins. There is one more junction at the eighth mile: take the lower road, "West 3". Only a four-wheel drive vehicle with reasonably good clearance should be able to make it to mile 9. Watch out for fallen rocks and ditches that traverse the roadbed. We advise you to inquire locally as to road conditions. Logging roads deteriorate rapidly without maintenance.

HIKING TIME: It is two hours into Chapman Lake which is three miles from the top of the logging road. From mile 8 it will take you an additional 1-1/2 hours. Allow yourself equal time for the return hike.

For those who wish an even longer trek, a sign has been posted along the trail indicating the route into Tannis Lake. McNair Lake is a twenty minute hike south-east from Chapman Lake. As these routes are not flagged you should consult a topographical map of the area.

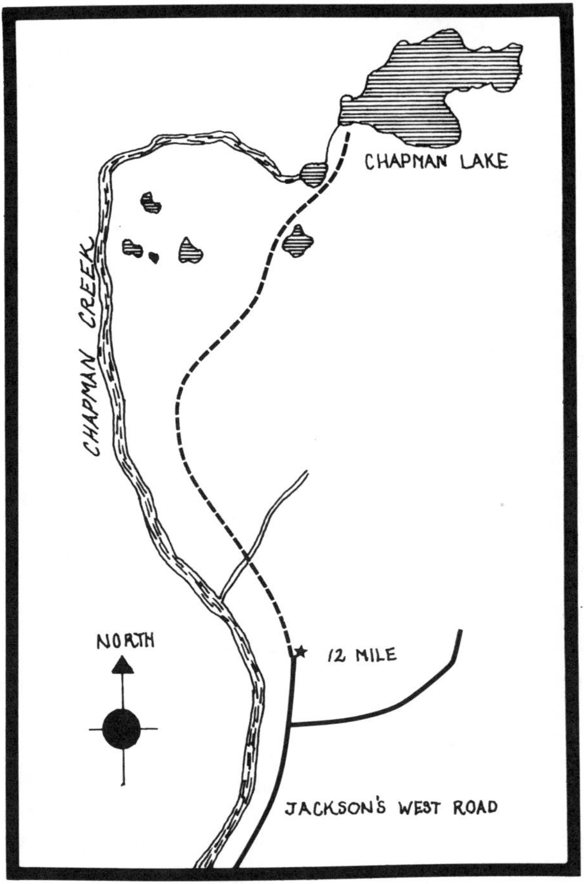
CHAPMAN LAKE
CHAPMAN CREEK
NORTH
12 MILE
JACKSON'S WEST ROAD

CHAPMAN LAKE

DESCRIPTION: Intermediate to Advanced. Running through an impressive stand of timber, this trail has been well marked with surveyors' tape. Several small streams are crossed and two lakes are passed before Chapman Lake is reached. In late fall, winter, and early spring snow may make the trail harder to follow. Snowshoes might be the best footwear. The elevation of Chapman Lake is 3500 feet and if you inquire at the forestry office in Sechelt they will be able to tell you approximately how much snow to expect at that elevation.

POINTS OF INTEREST: The forest through which this trail takes you in itself makes the hike worthwhile. The soft moss floor, numerous delicate lakes and ponds add to the attraction. Chapman Lake is a large cold lake and even in the heat of summer one can sometimes sunbathe on an ice floe. The magnificent, towering form of Panther Peak reigns to the south-east. This is one of those untouched wilderness areas that causes you to doubt the reality of towns and cities.

HAZARDS: Inquire at Jackson Bros. Logging office, or at the Sechelt Forestry Station, to make sure this logging road is not in use. A fully loaded logging truck barrelling down the mountain side cannot stop and in many places the road is too narrow for vehicles to pass or pull over!

Approach to Panther Peak with Chapman Lake in background. John
Harper photo.

JACKSON BROS. LOGGING ROADS

ACCESS: Take Highway 101 east from Sechelt to the Jackson Bros. Logging office in Wilson Creek. Across the highway, to the east of the Homestead Drive-In, is Jacksons' Logging Road. There is a large sign at the road entrance which reads "Logging Road Do Not Enter" ...this is the road you take.

HIKING TIME: Depending on how far you drive and how far you hike you can spend from one hour to several days enjoying these roads. The length of the West Road is twelve miles, and the East Road is thirteen miles. See the map for distances en route to specific spots.

DESCRIPTION: Primary to Advanced. For the periods when these roads are not in active use, fallen rock and streams washing across the roadbed can quickly make them impassable for any but four-wheel drive vehicles. But you can hike them for the next hundred years to your heart's content. The West Road is also the access route for the preceding Chapman Lake hike.

Meeting a logging truck barrelling down the road can be one of the most hair-raising experiences we know of! Before you decide to motor off, please inquire as to whether these roads are in use.

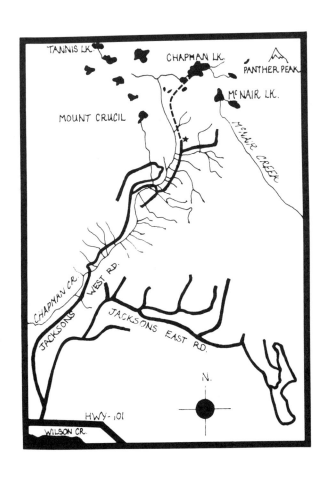

JACKSON'S LOGGING ROADS

POINTS OF INTEREST: Jacksons' West Road follows Chapman Creek up, crossing it in several places and running right alongside it in others. For fishing or just picnicking this creek is ideal; bring a rod, a sandwich and a friend. The East Road winds along the slopes of Mount Elphinstone, with dozens of spur roads leading into old slash areas. These roads are used primarily by hunters after deer and grouse, so leave your moose whistle at home during hunting season or you could be in trouble. From the eastern most reaches a splendid view of the Sunshine Coast, Howe Sound, and the Strait of Georgia can be seen.

HAZARDS: As mentioned earlier, if you are going to drive on these roads make sure there are no logging trucks in the area!

Mount Tetrahedron from Panther Peak. John Harper photo.

Howe Sound from Mount Elphinstone. John Hind-Smith photo.

CLIFF GILKER PARK

ACCESS: Take Highway 101 west from Gibsons approximately seven miles. The Recreation Site borders the Golf Course on the Gibsons side. A sign marking the entrance road is visible from the highway.

HIKING TIME: Ten minutes to two hours depending on the trails you choose.

DESCRIPTION: Primary. These trails meander through a park-like forest with representative varieties of trees, ferns, and other plant life local to the west coast rain forest.

POINTS OF INTEREST: Leisure Falls, Shadow Falls, and Basalt Gorge are lovely spots and rustic cedar bridges cross the creek at these locations. Picnic tables and campfire facilities are located in two places beside the creek and there is an outdoor amphitheatre for informal gatherings. An annual fall fair is held here in September with various craft and home-cooked goodie booths set up along the trails.

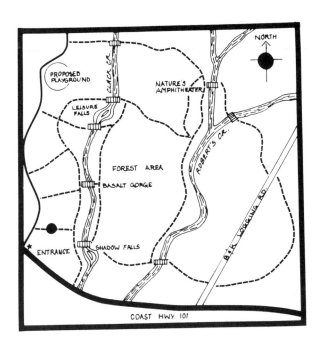

CLIFF GILKER PARK
(Formerly called "Recreation Site")

Cliff Gilker Park. John Hind-Smith photo.

Footbridge, Cliff Gilker Park. John Hind-Smith photo.

THE SHAKECUTTERS MEADOW

ACCESS: From highway 101 turn right onto Largo Road, locally known as 'the old B & K road', just east of the golf course. The condition of this road varies but you should have no trouble getting the family heap up to the powerline right-of-way. Follow Largo Road for about 50 minutes walking time until a newer logging road becomes visible traversing the hillside above. Climb up through the short alder covered embankment onto this second road and follow it uphill in a westerly direction keeping left until the shakecutters meadow appears below the road, curving in toward the mountain.

HIKING TIME: Approximately 2½ hours to reach the meadow, slightly less coming back.

DESCRIPTION: Intermediate. The roads are clear enough to follow and make for pleasant walking but its fairly long and the climb from the road down into the valley is steepish.

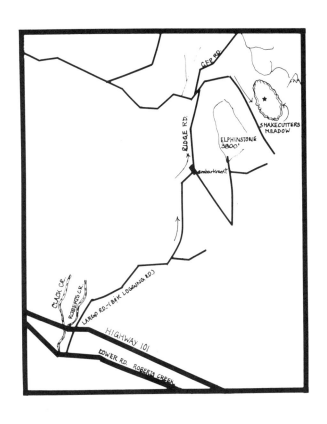

SHAKECUTTER'S MEADOW

POINTS OF INTEREST: In the early season, mid-June, this beautiful meadow is one of the best places to see such alpine flora as marsh marigold, gentian, wild orchid, yellow violets and later, asters, queen's cup, wild ginger and at least three different kinds of blueberry. Look also for alpine fir and true mountain ash.

Early in the century Japanese shakecutters used this meadow as the source for a long flume running downhill to tidewater. The meadow itself was used as a pasture for their mules and ditches and watering holes cut into the peat of the bog.

C. Bailey photo.

CEMETERY TRAIL

ACCESS: Take North Road from Gibsons and turn left at the end of the long straight stretch onto Cemetery Road. Then turn right on Gilmour Road and follow the road to the hydro line. The trail begins on the left, above the hydro line and gravel pit, behind the cablevision shed. Follow the cable line up the hill.

HIKING TIME: Approximately one and a half hours to the first receiver station and another half hour to the second receiver station which is two miles from the cablevision shed. The hiking time back is considerably less as you are following the trail almost straight down the mountain. Don't trip!

DESCRIPTION: Intermediate to Advanced. This trail follows the cablevision line through the woods, up Mount Elphinstone, and across an old slash area. Shake-cutter's trails intersect the cablevision trail at various points, and as we have not marked them all on the map it is essential that you follow the cable line at all junctions.

The moss-covered forest floor gives way to wild blueberry bushes at higher elevations; a favorite snack for summer bears. We also saw some chillingly large cougar tracks when we were up in the snow.

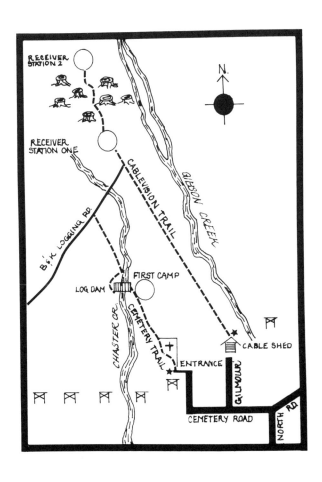

CEMETERY & CABLEVISION TRAILS

The remains of the first shake-cutters' camp can be seen at the first level spot you come to, on the south side of Chaster Creek. Most of the intact pottery and tools have long since fallen to the treasure hunters, but an industrious digger may still find something.

Supplies for the camps were brought from Gibsons by horse to a tramway which began just below the cemetery. From there the supplies were hauled up to first camp, and remnants of this tramway can still be seen to the east of the trail. The huge flywheel from the tramway's gas engine is located fifty feet west of the trail, just below first camp.

A flume was constructed to carry the shake bolts from first camp down to what is now the Langdale ferry terminal. From here barges carried the bolts to Vancouver markets. The water necessary for this flume was held in a pool behind a log dam that shake-cutters built on Chaster Creek. This dam is still intact and the cleared area around it makes a good spot for picnicking. Some innovative wayfarer has even constructed a lecture stand here, though for what purpose remains unknown.

From Chaster Creek a second tramway ran up to second camp. This tramway, used to carry shingle bolts down to the flume, has suffered less decay than the lower one, and can be followed right up to the B. & K. Logging Road.

Today the Sunshine Coast still supports a large shake industry, though more modern methods are used. Several of the old-time loggers we talked with remembered that bygone era with a shake of the head and a smile.

Remains of shinglebolt flume on Mount Elphinstone. Fred W. Inglis photo. ▶

CABLEVISION TRAIL

ACCESS: Take North Road from Gibsons and turn left onto Cemetery Road. Follow the road to the gate at the end. See map to avoid taking a wrong turning on private drives.

HIKING TIME: Less than one-half hour to first camp, another forty-five minutes to B. & K. Logging Road; which is 1-1/4 miles from the gate. From the end of Cemetery Trail at B. & K., it is only a ten-minute walk east to the Cablevision Trail. See the Cablevision Trail map and description if you would like to take a circuit route rather than returning by the same trail. Watch for the overhead cable marking the Cablevision's Trail intersection with B. & K. Road.

DESCRIPTION: Intermediate to Advanced. From the first level spot one-half mile up, follow the trail to the left, from which point on it is marked with surveyor's tags. The latter half of the trail follows the old tramway directly up the mountain. If you lose sight of the tags just follow the tramway.

POINTS OF INTEREST: The historical significance of this trail is one of its main features and researching its background was one of our more rewarding tasks.

At the close of World War One a major shake-cutting operation was run on Mount Elphinstone. The many men this operation employed lived in two camps on the mountain.

Log bridge, Mount Elphinstone. John Hind-Smith photo. ▶

This trip can also be used as part of the circuit route in combination with the preceding Cemetery Trail.

POINTS OF INTEREST: Half a mile up the trail stand the remains of an old wooden flume which was built just after World War One. The flume was used to float shakes from the shake camp down the mountain to what is now the Langdale ferry terminal and from there they were barged to Vancouver. We have included a fuller outline of this operation in the preceding notes on Cemetery Trail.

From the first receiver station just above the slash line you can see Howe Sound, the coastline, and the many islands to the south. From the second receiver station the town of Gibsons and a panoramic view of Vancouver Island can be seen. The extra half-hour climb is worth it!

HAZARDS: Do not tamper with the cablevision line.

(For map see Cemetery Trail)

Remains of shakecutters' tramway, Mount Elphinstone. John Hind-Smith photo.

SOAMES HILL
(THE KNOB)

ACCESS: Follow Marine Drive from Gibsons 1-1/2 miles toward Langdale. Take the first road on your left past Feeney Road. It is a wide gravel road cutting back at an angle and is marked with a sign reading "Soames Hill Park". This access route is for climbing up the front of the Knob.

For access up the back of the Knob, take Chamberlin Road off North Road, then take Bridgeman Road off Chamberlin. At the first curve in Bridgeman Road the access road, marked with a sign, heads into the Knob.

HIKING TIME: Twenty minutes up the front, and fifteen minutes up the back, though the back is an easier route. More signs near the base of the knob indicate the route around the bottom joining the two trails. This joining route only takes ten minutes.

DESCRIPTION: Primary. A stiff leg's guess would put the number of stairs toiling up this hill at too many! As can be seen from the perspective our mapmaker chose to illustrate it, this trail is a mean one. But then on the other hand it doesn't take that long to climb up.

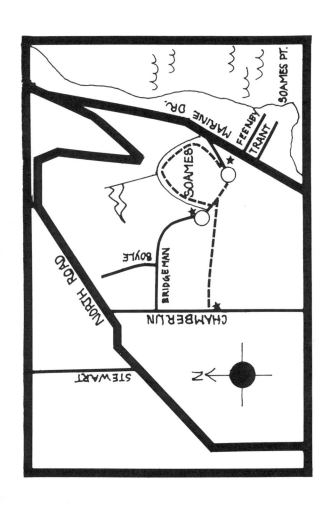

SOAMES HILL

POINTS OF INTEREST: After the buildup in the last paragraph we'd better give you a reason for torturing your calf muscles up this one: there is a splendid view. Howe Sound with all the islands, the Squamish mountain range, and even Point Grey, are all visible, and the village of Gibsons is at your feet.

The cedar bough hand railings and fallen logs with stairs cut into them are also intriguing and help to take your mind off the ascent. Shades of climbing the Great Pyramids.

For those who have more important things to do than climb hills, a shady clearing near the base of the knob offers a quaint cedar bench.

HAZARDS: The knob is extremely steep and drops almost straight off at the top viewpoints. At this time there are no guard rails to spoil the view or catch the unwary.

Beachcomber country: View of Gibsons from the Knob (Soames Hill).
Author photo.

Log stairway leading up Soames Hill. Author photo.

GAMBIER LAKE

ACCESS: Gambier Island is a fifteen minute ferry ride aboard the thirty foot M.V. Dogwood Princess. This little foot-passenger ferry stops first at Gambier harbour and then carries on another fifteen minutes to New Brighton where our hike begins. Should you get off at the first stop you will find yourself faced with an extra mile walk over to New Brighton.

At this time the first ferry leaving Langdale for Gambier is at 7:40 a.m., and if you are to complete this hike in time to catch the last ferry back at 6:45 p.m., this is your boat. Please check current sailing schedules before you go as B.C. Ferries has a habit of changing these schedules at whim.

HIKING TIME: 3-1/2 - 4 hours into Gambier Lake which is 5-3/8 miles from New Brighton. Slightly less time for the return as most of it is downhill. Rather than rushing in and out again to connect with ferries why not camp overnight at the lake? It's a good spot.

DESCRIPTION: Intermediate to Advanced. New Brighton, named after its English counterpart, has an old world flavour in its country lanes. It also has the only Legion Hall we know of where they still sing "God Save the Queen" at midnight.

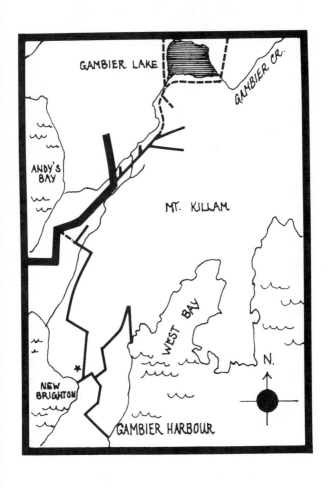

GAMBIER LAKE

A couple of miles out of New Brighton the road is blocked by a chain. From here you take the trail to your left which takes you over half a mile of corduroy road; a road that was handbuilt by laying logs side by side along the roadbed to produce a corrugated or corduroy effect. This kept vehicles from becoming caught in the mud underneath the logs. This trail will bring you out on the main logging road, where you turn right, up the hill.

Once you leave the main logging road at mile 3-1/8 you must watch for slash marks on trees to show you the right road at all major forks. We have not drawn in all the smaller, more overgrown spur roads on the map so do check your map closely to make sure you are on the right heading.

After the fifth mile the old logging road gives way to a trail which descends to the lake. A stream runs down this trail making it extremely slippery, and all those white and seemingly dry shingle slabs are treacherous.

Around the north-eastern edge of Gambier Lake is a gravelly beach beside a stream, with lots of room for camping. The road does continue on from here but it runs through private property down to a (church) camp on the ocean.

HAZARDS: That streambed down to the lake is slipperier than it looks.

HIKING, HIKING, AND MORE HIKING

For further information on these hikes contact the local Forestry Office for maps and information.

HYDRO LINE

Primary to Advanced. You can hike from one end of the coast to the other by following the hydro line. You may have to ford the odd ravine or creek.

JOHNSON LOGGING ROAD

Intermediate to Advanced. On the highway from Langdale to Port Melon this road takes off and runs back up for miles. Higher up it offers a good view; with one fork heading up Mount Elphinstone.

DAKOTA CREEK

Intermediate to Advanced. The road for the Dakota Creek hike also comes off the Port Melon highway. Remains of an old flume used in a shake operation can be seen literally hanging on the sides of a gorge. There is a place to camp at the top and rumours of an abandoned gold mine...

LANGDALE FALLS

Intermediate. Langdale Creek is the one that comes out at the Langdale ferry terminal; the falls are several miles up. You can start up from the terminal, following the road on the north bank of the creek until it crosses the creek, and then continuing up the creekbed on your own. There is also a trail starting behind the garbage dump on Stewart Road but it is mainly overgrown and beyond mapping.

DOYLE'S LOGGING ROADS

Intermediate to Advanced. One of the areas longest logging road systems, this one starts in Halfmoon Bay, goes right up over the mountains and down into Sechelt Inlet. Carlson Lake, Lyons Lake, and Doyle Lake are along the way. The view from the top is fine and so are the alpine meadows.

MIDDLEPOINT LOGGING ROADS

Intermediate to Advanced. Starting in the Pender Harbour area, this network of roads winds over the hills behind, with the usual views, creeks, and wildlife that make the coast so memorable.

McNAB CREEK

Advanced. Several miles past the Port Melon mill this logging road goes up over the mountains and down into Salmon Inlet. It's a good fifteen-mile hike one way and even in late spring snow may be encountered at the higher elevations. As there is no road connecting Port Melon and McNab Creek you must go by boat or hike the extra distance.

McNAIR LAKE

Intermediate to Advanced. Starting up the logging road opposite the gravel pit on the highway before Port Melon and then switching to a trail after several miles, this hike can be gruelling. Several years ago a trail was cut and flagged but it is almost totally overgrown with devils club, a fierce deterent to even the hardiest.

RAINY RIVER

Intermediate to Advanced. Just past Port Melon this old logging road climbs up to a small but lovely lake on the Rainy River. A dam on the lake is controlled from Port Melon, which uses the water in its mill operations.

THE TANTALUS RANGE

For further information on this hike contact Barb Laakso at 885-9617. Barb has hiked this route and has much valuable information on the specifics of hiking this area.

For maps and current weather conditions contact the Sechelt Forestry Office.

This hike, taking four to five days one way, starts in Wilson Creek at Jacksons Brothers Logging Road and ends at Woodfibre.

From Jacksons West Road all the way up to Tetrahedron Mountain the going is reasonably easy, as there is road and then trail most of the way.

Past Tetrahedron there is no trail, and the gullies of Sechelt Creek and McNab Creek must be crossed. There is a way through the Sechelt Creek gully but specific information is necessary for McNab Creek gully as it is mainly steep cliffs on either side.

At Woodfibre there is a ferry running over to Darrell Bay, just past Brittania Beach on the Squamish highway.

This hike runs through the Tantalus Mountain Range, with Tetrahedron, Mount Elphinstone, and Panther Peak along the coast and the snowy tops of endless mountains stretching to the horizon behind. The elevation through here limits vegetation to scrubby trees and blueberries, though heavy underbrush may have to be dealt with crossing the two gullies.

CROSS-COUNTRY SKIING
ON THE SUNSHINE COAST

Even many local residents appear not to realize that the Sunshine Coast offers some of the best cross-country skiing to be found in this part of the province. There are two principal areas—the logging roads and open slopes around Mount Elphinstone in the southern part of the region and the logging slashes and roads of the high country above Halfmoon Bay and Pender Harbour in the northern part.

I.   THE MOUNT ELPHINSTONE AREA

Best access is once again, the Jackson Brothers logging road which runs north from Highway 101 at Wilson Creek. Take the east fork leading southeast toward Mount Elphinstone and drive up as far as snow conditions permit.

From the Tetrahedron Ski Club's warm-up trailer at Mile 6 to Mount Elphinstone the slope is gentle and makes a good warm-up run when the snow is down that far. At other times it may be possible to drive as far as Mile 10 near the base of the mountain.

There are numerous possibilities open to the skier from Mile 6 onward, even when the snow is not deep enough to make the logging slash skiable and he must stay to the roads. Some marking has been done by the Tetrahedron Ski Club but there are no groomed trails and it is largely up to the individual to go in whichever direction the spirit moves him. However there are some suggestions which can be made.

Elphinstone Ridge

This may be reached by continuing on the Jackson Brothers East Road to the Mile 12 marker and branching right onto the smaller road that leads up to the ridge. As you approach the crest you will see the old Tetrahedron ski tow that once serviced the open slope above it, and farther up the trail the small A-frame ski lodge maintained by the Tetrahedron Ski Club. This is a good spot to rest and mug up before trying the excellent alpine touring along the crest. Looking west there is an unsurpassed view of Georgia Strait and the coastline from Roberts Creek up past the White Islets to the Village of Sechelt with Lasqueti and Texada Islands in the background. Facing the A-frame, the 4,137-foot peak of Mount Elphinstone rises on the right and the waters of Howe Sound may be seen stretching towards Garibaldi far below. Still facing the A-frame and following the sweep of the bowl to the left, Panther Peak may be seen rising 5,500 feet in the distance. To the right of the A-frame skiers can climb the gentle slope into the trees and find ideal touring country with lookouts toward the city of Vancouver.

West Shoulder Run

Keep to the left at Mile 9 near the base of Mount Elphinstone. The west shoulder run is about a mile long and goes around the east side of the mountain. A gradual incline flattens out into good mountain touring after the first quarter mile. The right side of the road rises steeply into heavy timber while the left drops away over new logging slash. There is an avalanche track down the east side of the mountain about a mile along the run.

Dakota Bowl Run

Branch left from Jackson Brothers East Road at Mile 8. The road rises gradually for three-quarters of a mile, then flattens out, offering good skiing for the next 2¼ miles. Three miles in from the junction with Jackson Brothers East Road is a washed-out bridge just before the road turns to the left up towards the treeline. Hiking through the trees at the end of the road one may reach more open sub-alpine terrain which makes for beautiful touring but should be attempted only by experienced cross-country skiers travelling with company and good equipment. It takes a good day to get in and out of this area and the unmarked trails are easy to confuse.

II.   THE NORTHERN AREA (SECHELT PENINSULA)

The access to this area is gained by leaving Highway 101 at Halfmoon Bay and travelling north up the Trout Lake Road about half a mile to the intersection with Doyle's logging road. Once again this is an active logging road and caution must be used to avoid trucks except during the winter shutdown period.

There are probably a hundred miles of new and old logging roads up in this country and the choice has to be made early on which general area is to be attempted. One can go to the left side of the Caren Range, along its ridge, or turn right and go down towards Snake Bay on Sechelt Inlet. There is good skiing to be found along either route but once you've taken one of them you can't switch without coming back almost to your starting point. Much of this area is logged-off and open but there are also extensive areas in second growth and more suitable for snow-shoeing.

Safety Precautions

It can be assumed that most skiers are aware of the basic safety aspects of the sport but it may not be out of place to point out that anyone venturing into unfamiliar country should find out as much as possible about the area beforehand. The best general map available is the Provincial Government topographical map Section 92 G/12 covering Sechelt Inlet but even here only the main logging roads are shown. A compass is a must in this country, as are extra warm clothing, dry socks, waterproof matches, a knife and an extra ski tip. It is also highly advisable to tell someone back in civilization which general area you intend visiting along with your estimated time of return. This is obvious advice but it is too often neglected.

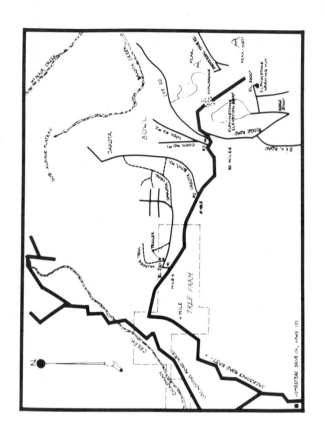

MOUNT ELPHINSTONE SKI AREA

Tetrahedron Ski Club

This club is active only in the Mount Elphinstone area, where it has done some work in marking trails, establishing the warm-up trailer and building the A-frame ski hut on Elphinstone Ridge. It has had its ups and downs in past but seems to have come through them now and plans many trips to serve all types of skiers, both cross-country and downhill. The club does not have a permanent phone but anyone interested can contact them either by asking around or contacting the Coast News in Gibsons.

Rick Crosby and John Hind-Smith

EMERGENCY NUMBERS

	Fire	Police	Ambulance
Gibsons	886-2345	886-2245	886-2121
Pender Harbour	883-2345	885-2266	883-2764
Port Melon	884-5222	886-2245	886-2121
Roberts Creek	885-3222	886-2245	886-2121
Sechelt	885-2345	885-2266	885-9927

PROVINCIAL PARKS

PLUMPER COVE MARINE PARK is a lovely campsite on Keats Island, a 1-mile boat trip from Gibsons harbour.

ROBERTS CREEK PARK encompasses two separate areas. The main area, on highway 101, has 25 units for camping. 3/4 mile south-east of the camping area is a picnic ground at the beach, connected to the main area by road.

PORPOISE BAY PARK is a new 150-acre campground just north of Sechelt and has become the most popular park on the Sunshine Coast. It has a long sandy beach for swimming, 89 campsites, and full facilities. Angus Creek on the north edge of the park offers a fascinating show in the fall when coho and chum salmon return to spawn, and a pleasant trail meanders down its shady banks.

SMUGGLERS COVE MARINE PARK is a 450-acre park just now being developed for campers, though it has been a favorite with boaters for years. The hike into the park is listed earlier in this book.

GARDEN BAY MARINE PARK is on the north shore of Pender Harbour at Garden Bay, with frontage on the ocean at Garden Bay and on Garden Bay Lake. It includes Mount Daniel which has been listed earlier in this book. This park is totally undeveloped.

SKOOKUMCHUCK NARROWS PARK is a 100-acre park centreing around the amazing Skookumchuck rapids on Sechelt Inlet. While camping is not permitted here, the spectacle of the rapids makes the short hike in worthwhile. At the narrows the waters of the Pacific Ocean are constricted as they ebb and flow each day. As the tide forces through the narrows it boils and churns with a roar that can be heard for miles. These rapids occur four times a day, twice on the ebb and twice on the flow.

PRINCESS LOUISA MARINE PARK is accessible by boat only and a regular run there is offered by Buccaneer Marina of Secret Cove during summer months. This 100-acre park has basic camping facilities and floats for boaters. Chatterbox Falls are one of the highlights of this beautiful inlet park.

RECREATION APPENDIX

TRANSPORTATION FACILITIES

B.C. Ferries run daily from Horseshoe Bay to Langdale, Langdale to Gambier Island, and Earl's Cove to Saltery Bay. Langdale terminal 886-2242.

Tyee Airways, situated in Porpoise Bay, flies regularly from Sechelt to Vancouver, Nanaimo and Pender Harbour. Planes may also be Chartered for access to remote localities and for sightseeing. 885-2214.

Sechelt Motor Transportation runs buses twice daily from the Vancouver bus depot through to Powell River, with stops all along the highway. Sechelt depot 885-2217.

PUBLIC SERVICES

Tourist Information 885-3100
Fisheries Department 883-2313
Conservation Officer 885-2004
Forestry Office 885-2034
Parks Branch 885-9019

NOTES